W9-AMV-385

Leaving a Mark

Illustrated by
Tim Hodge

Nicole DeRosa Cannella
with Dorian "D-Strong" Murray

Lampion Press, LLC
P. O. Box 932
Silverton, OR 97381

ISBN: 978-1-942614-15-9

Library of Congress Control Number: 2016932788

Photo credit for Ms. Cannella: Jaclyn Tillinghast, Jaclyn.Photography.com

Photo credit for Dorian Murray: Binkeez for Comfort

Formatting and cover design: Amy Cole, JPL Design Solutions

Printed in the United States of America

Dedication

Everyone longs to leave a mark in this world.

Big or little, quiet or loud, we all long to leave a legacy. That is what "being famous" should achieve; leaving a mark and a legacy that blesses and enriches people's lives. It is our prayer that this book, and Dorian's words, will do just that—leave a mark of hope that shines bright in an otherwise dark time. We dedicate this story to Dorian, all who love him, and to children everywhere who are facing cancer with hope in their hearts and a peace that speaks louder than fear. Our intent is that they can hold this story close, find comfort in it, and know that they are loved. We thank all of the contributors who believed in and prayed for this project to come to fruition and all of you who, through your purchase, are aiding in the effort to end this disease. Remember, this can be a time of beginnings, not endings.

Below are other great opportunities to donate with the goal of offering help and finding a cure:

www.danafarberbostonchildrens.org
www.stjude.org
www.pmc.org
www.standup2cancer.org
www.stbaldricks.org
www.hasbrochildrenshospital.org
www.loveyourmelon.com
www.binkeezforcomfort.org

And for more information, visit www.cancer.org.

An encouraging word from

Dorian "D-Strong" Murray

"Don't be afraid;
you can be a champion too.
Always believe in yourself and
never give up!"

~Dorian

I may have lost my hair–
but I didn't lose my courage–
did you know that in one's fear,
so much strength can flourish?

I'm just a little kid, you see–
but forced to handle cancer,
I had dreams of being fancy things–
like an actor or a dancer.

But what I thought would bring me fame,
like those cool jobs I mentioned–
couldn't bring this kind of strength,
or extraordinary friendships.

You see, through this awful cancer news–
great stuff has poured through,
like discovering I have super power,
and making friends so true.

When I have to take the medicines
that in the end should help,
they can make me feel so terrible,
and definitely not myself.

But there are kids just like me–
that have to take them too,
one of them walked up to me
saying, "I'm Sam, who are you?"

4

That's how we make best friends,
in places like the hospital–
and how our super strength gets tested,
and we see how people are thoughtful.

Strangers we have never met
send things like books and hats;
soft blankets we can wear when we
feel cold or really sad.

The kids I've met look just like me–
most have lost their hair,
and those who haven't lost their's yet,
we meet, and show we care.

The meds I take make me feel weird–
sometimes I hate them so,
I want to flush them down the toilet
and yell "See ya!" as they go.

At times they make me dizzy
or have a stomach ache–
some make my head feel fuzzy,
and some can make me shake.

But this, I trust, that they can help–
they just might do the trick,
of helping wipe my cancer clean–
so I'll no longer be sick.

At times I get so angry,
and feel like it's unfair–
I shake my fists and stomp my feet,
and shout into the air.

I say things like "Why me?"
and when there's no reply–
I remind myself to breathe
and force myself to try...

...try to stay brave and to be strong–
and on days that I cannot,
my mom or dad, they hold me tight–
and say my back, they've got.

And speaking about bravery–
you should meet my family,
sometimes I feel it's worse on them;
because to deal with this is scary.

I long to cheer all of them up,
to assure them I'm ok...
but none of us can seem to find–
just the right words to say.

Cancer may have left its mark,
with needles, bumps and bruises–
but I will leave my mark on earth
in whatever way God chooses.

13

I've gotten sort of used to
this new bald head of mine–
It's not what's on the outside that counts,
but my spirit that makes me shine.

People often look away–
or worse, they kind of stare,
they say things like "Oh, you poor thing…"
perhaps because they care.

Maybe they mean well. I don't know–
but it makes my parents sad.
They'd rather people build me up
and say words to make me glad.

Moms and Dads–
if your kids ask me a cancer question,
please don't punish them as if it's wrong,
they ask with good intentions.

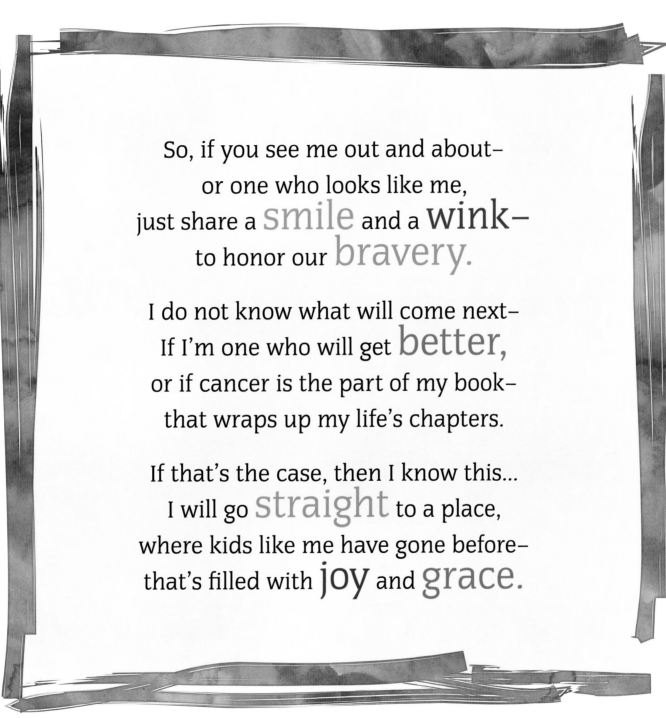

So, if you see me out and about–
or one who looks like me,
just share a smile and a wink–
to honor our bravery.

I do not know what will come next–
If I'm one who will get better,
or if cancer is the part of my book–
that wraps up my life's chapters.

If that's the case, then I know this...
I will go straight to a place,
where kids like me have gone before–
that's filled with joy and grace.

And there my body will be brand new–
no more sickness and pain,
I'll meet the One who created me–
I know He knows my name.

But I'm not quite ready to go there yet–
I have much more to do,
so, that's why I'm fighting with all I've got—
and why I wrote for you.

I want kids all over the world–
to know how strong they are,
to understand they're not alone;
and they're a shining star.

It's true, that we may never meet–
unless it is in Heaven,
your name could be Kate, or Sage, or Dorian–
or Nicholas or Kevin.

What matters is that we have a sickness
that bonds us as close friends–
and that no matter where life leads...

This is the beginning...

NOT
The End.

Afterword

I wasn't prepared for this.

At all.

I'll bet you weren't either. Nothing can prepare a parent for the news that their baby is fighting a battle for their life.

Maybe the news came in the emergency room, or from your child's pediatrician, it really doesn't matter. You think your child is sick; maybe it's something more serious than a cold or growing pains, but when the doctor walks into the room with that look on their face, you just know it's something more. They tell you something you will never, ever forget for as long as you live...

"I'm so sorry, your child has cancer."

Time stops, your body freezes and your mind refuses to believe what you just heard.

The very first thing every cancer parent thinks is "This can't be happening. What is going to happen to my baby?" Just like that you have entered into the Cancer World and you better hang on tight, because you are going for a crazy ride.

What is interesting about this crazy ride, is that it will be so scary and, well, something else too...your life has changed, regardless of whether you're the child who got the news, a parent to a child just diagnosed, another family member or a close friend—your lives are different now. The cancer journey will have its difficult times, but...
I want you to know, it WILL have good times too. You will make new friends!

Kids like you, parents like you, caregivers like you... you will connect with others going through exactly what you are and although you wish you had never had to meet these new friends, you will be forever thankful that you have.

Whether your crazy cancer journey has just started, is mid protocol, or coming to an end, you should know... you are doing a great job. You are amazing.

You are a fighter. You are strong. You are #DStrong.

Sending you light, love, and positivity.

Melissa

Melissa Murray
Mother to Dorian Murray
#DStrong

Acknowledgments

A very special thanks

are due to the many people who understood the vision and urgency of this book and worked behind the scenes to bring it to completion. We especially want to thank...

Chris Murray and family, the extended Doty and Murray families and the entire #DStrong support system, Sage and Liam Wallace, Jay Cannella, Nick, Olivia and Noelle Cannella, Sandy Hodge, Irina House, Elizabeth DeRosa, Jennifer Brown, Casey Rauda, Britni Spontelli, Amy Cole, Sandy Gould, Brad Rusticus, Gina Palmer, John Parenteau, Yvonne Masakowski, Maureen Sliney, Gerard DeRosa, Robert Reed, Melanie and Keith Lapointe, Anthony Michael Hall, Kate DeRosa, Robin Ivy. Special thanks to Deb Fezzuoglio who took a loving chance on a post, to Laura Wallace and Jim Menzies who worked selflessly to bring this to fruition, and to all who prayed for this project and believed in it.

We give thanks to the God of all mercy, comfort, and love.

About the Authors

Dorian "D-Strong" Murray was diagnosed with stage 4 cancer of the muscle tissue at age four. Now eight years old, he has defied the odds medically and in doing so, touched the world with his strength, wit and words. His wish to "be famous" in the city with that big "bridge," aka The Great Wall of China, was brought public by his parents who requested a response from anyone who was connected with the country. Instead, the world responded. From China, to Paris, America to Australia, celebrities, businesses, politicians and children just like Dorian, reached out with love in their hearts and signs in their hands to support #DStrong.

His wish to leave a legacy has indeed come true and with his indelible words in this book, he inspires yours to as well. Dorian lives in Rhode Island with his adoring family and enjoys Pokemon, Minions, pizza, baking and cooking.

Nicole DeRosa Cannella began her writing career with *The Ribbit Exhibit,* a children's book that explores bullying and compassion, soon to become a series. Her years of teaching and working in theatre, led her to combine her love of children and the arts into writing form; focusing on subjects that aren't always easy to discuss and presenting them in ways with which children can identify.

She received her BA in English Lit and Theatre in 1996. Her most valued role is raising three wonderful children alongside her husband. She lives in the Boston area, and is working on several writing projects. She feels blessed to have collaborated with Dorian and Melissa and prays that this book offers hope to children and their families facing pediatric cancer while aiding in the funding to eradicate it altogether.

About the Illustrator

 TimHodge is an animator, storyboard artist, animation director, illustrator and author. He has been in the animation industry for over twenty-five years, working on commercials, TV shows and feature films such as *The Lion King* and *Mulan.* Currently, he is directing episodes of the Big Idea series "VeggieTales in the House" appearing on Netflix. He lives in Tennessee with his family.